Bb

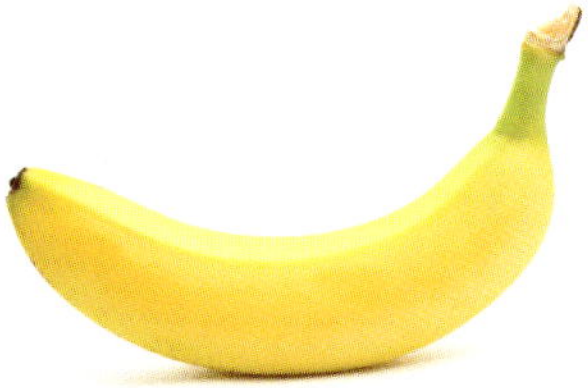

Ransom

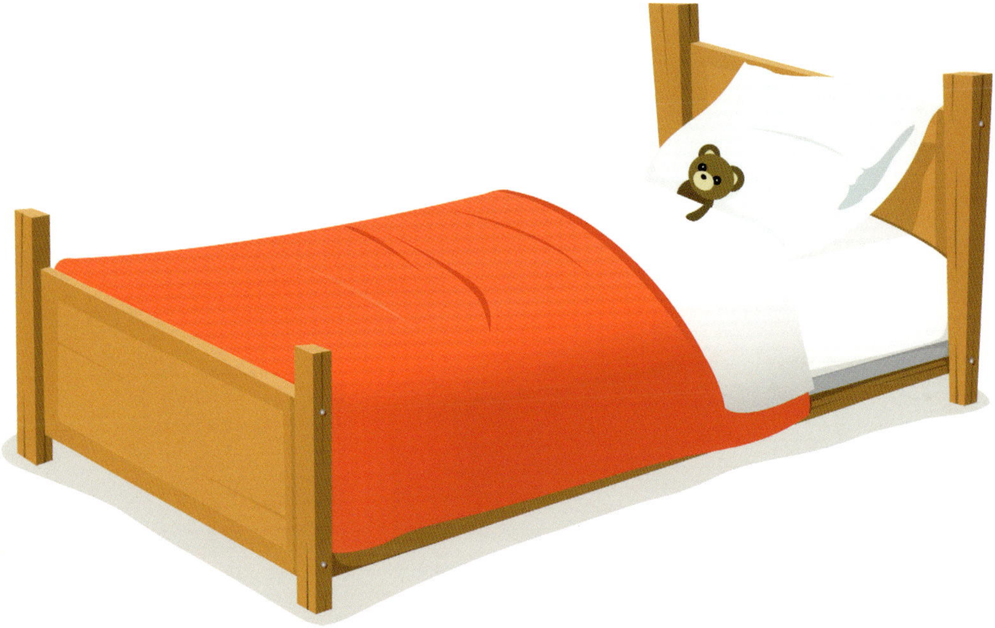

bed

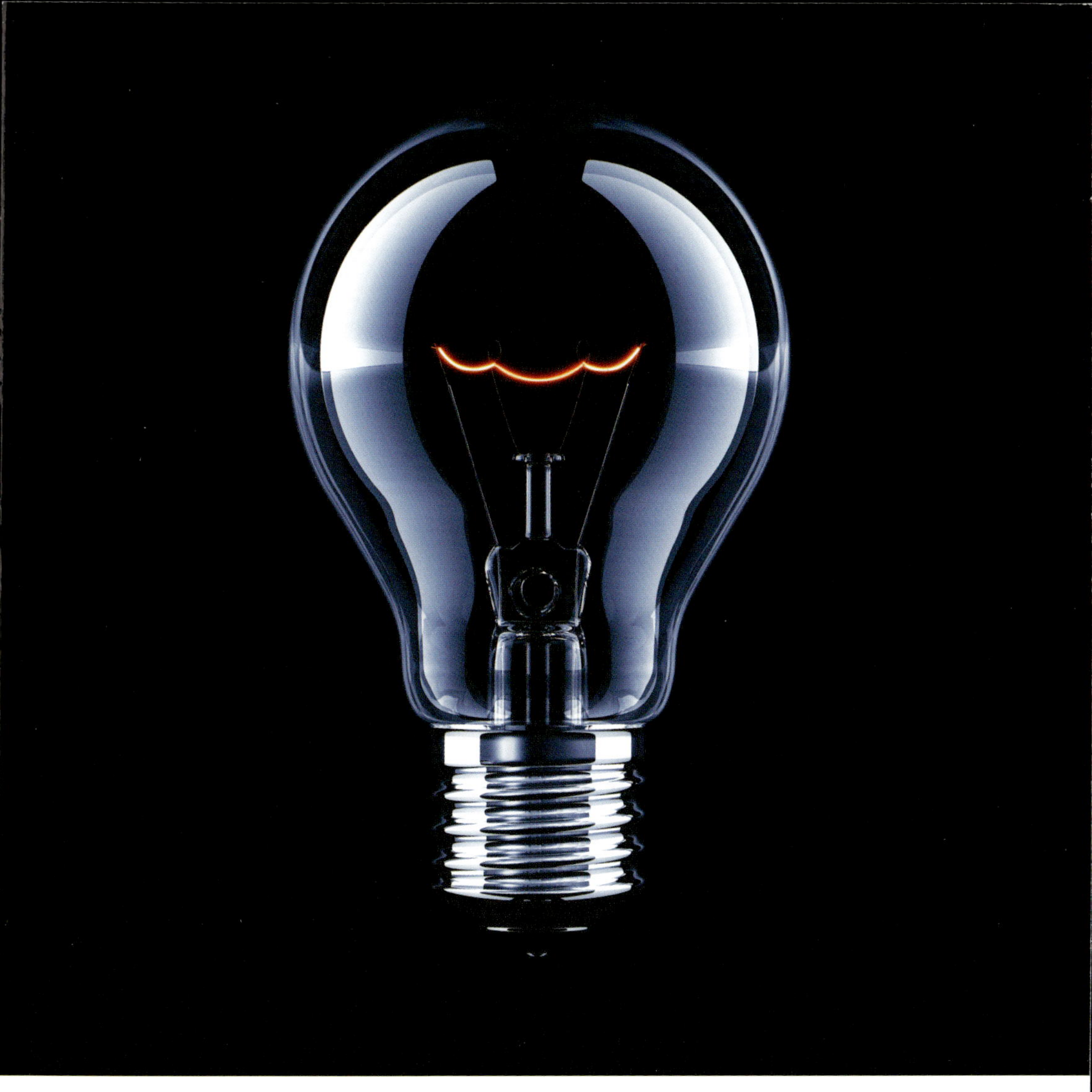

bulb

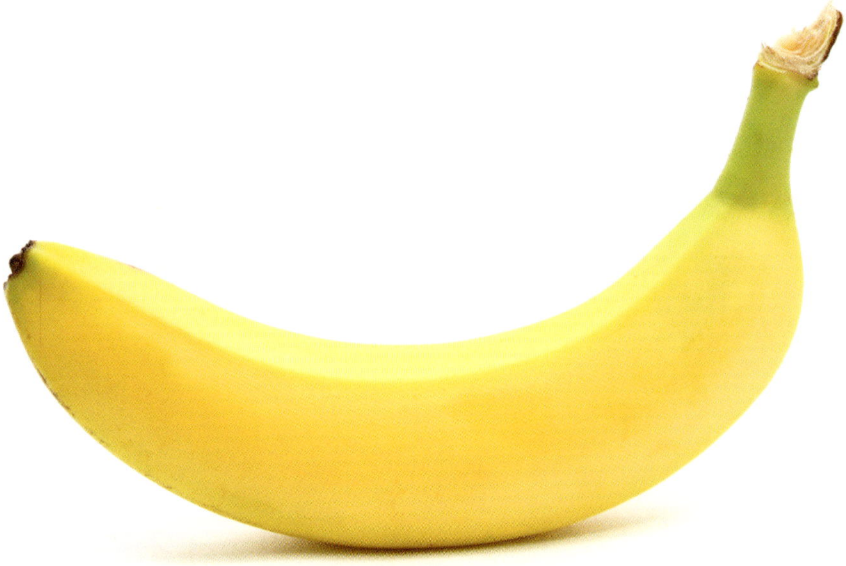

banana

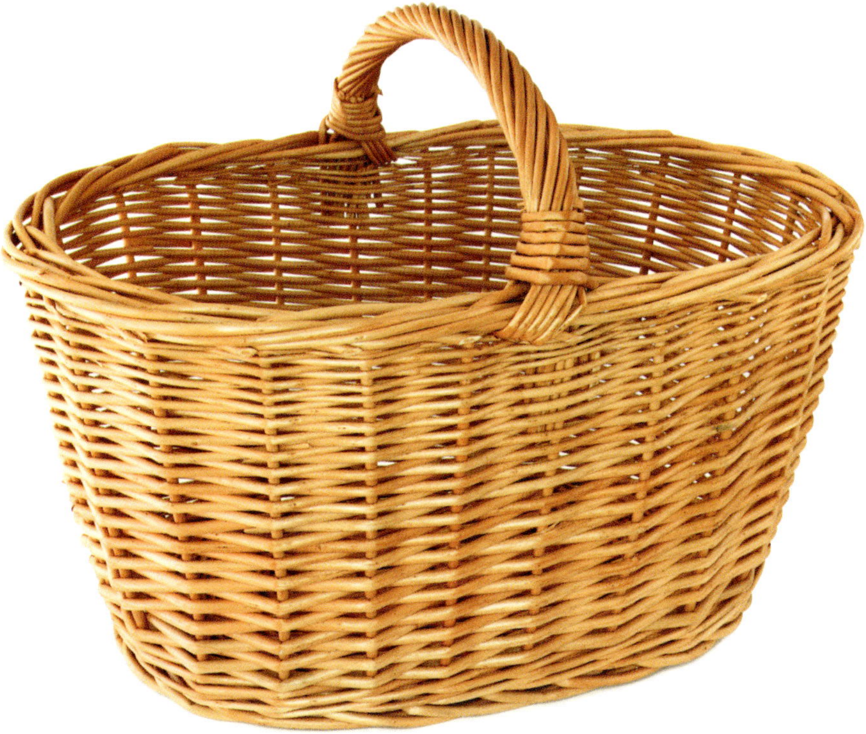

basket

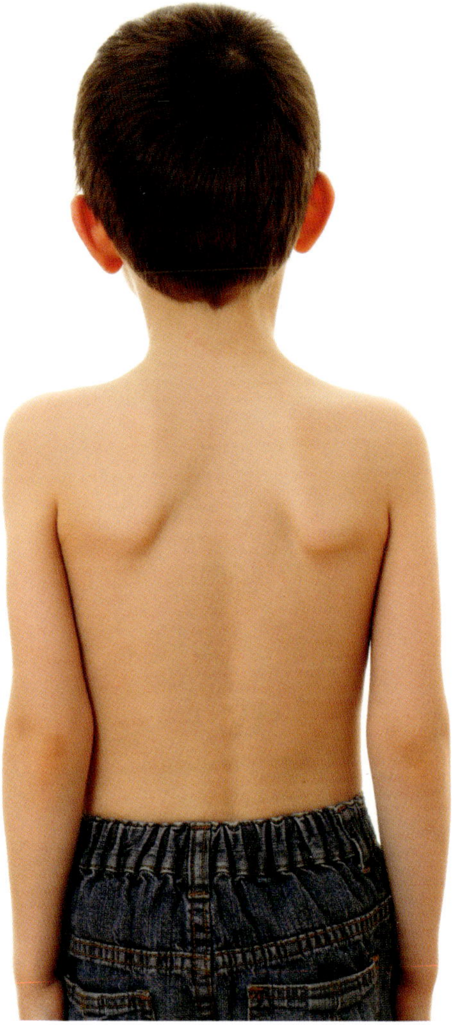

back

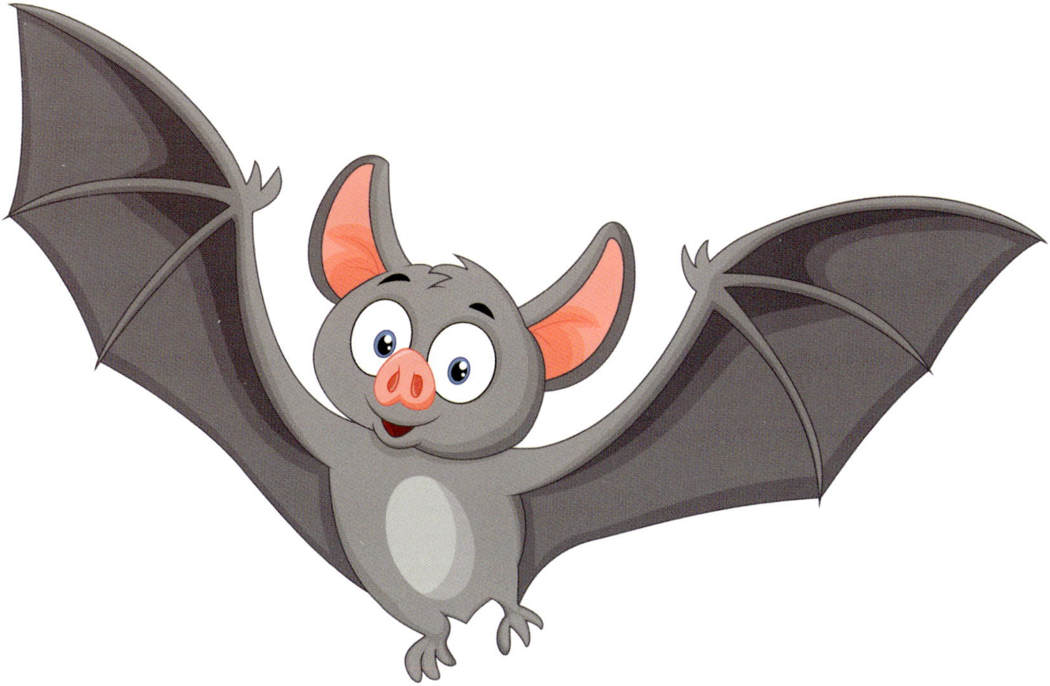

bat

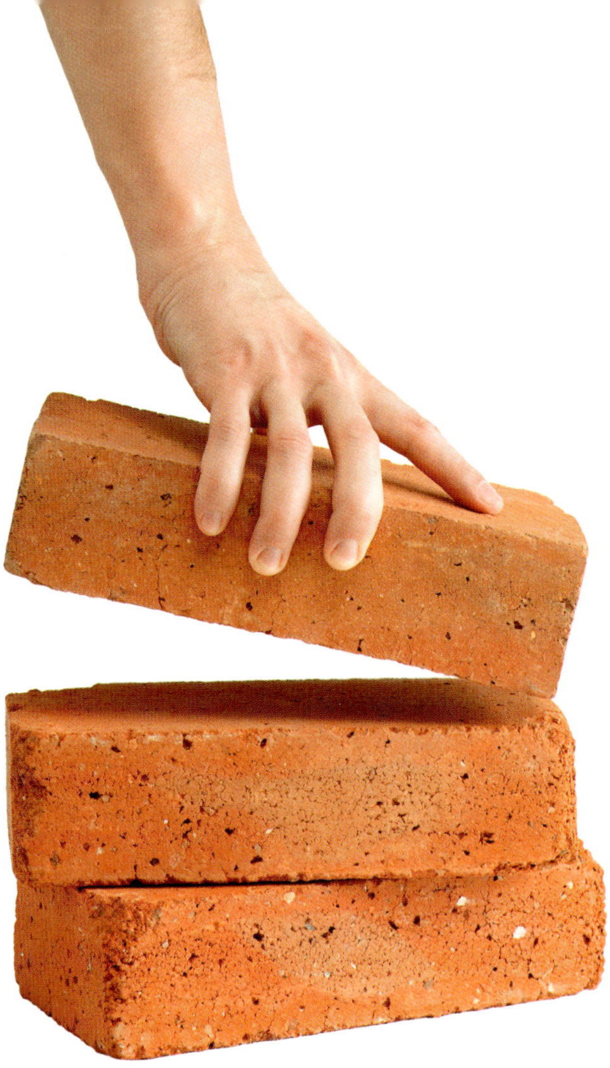

bricks

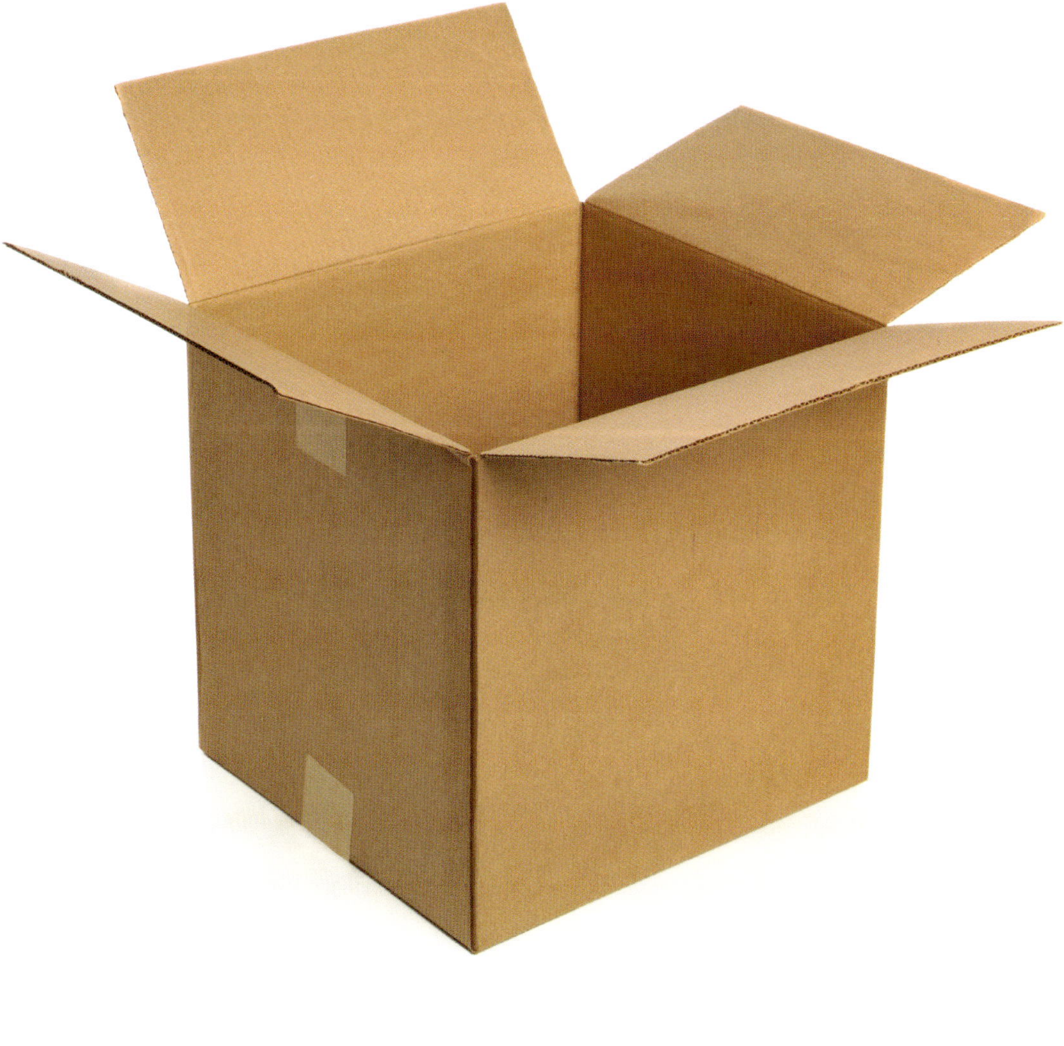

box

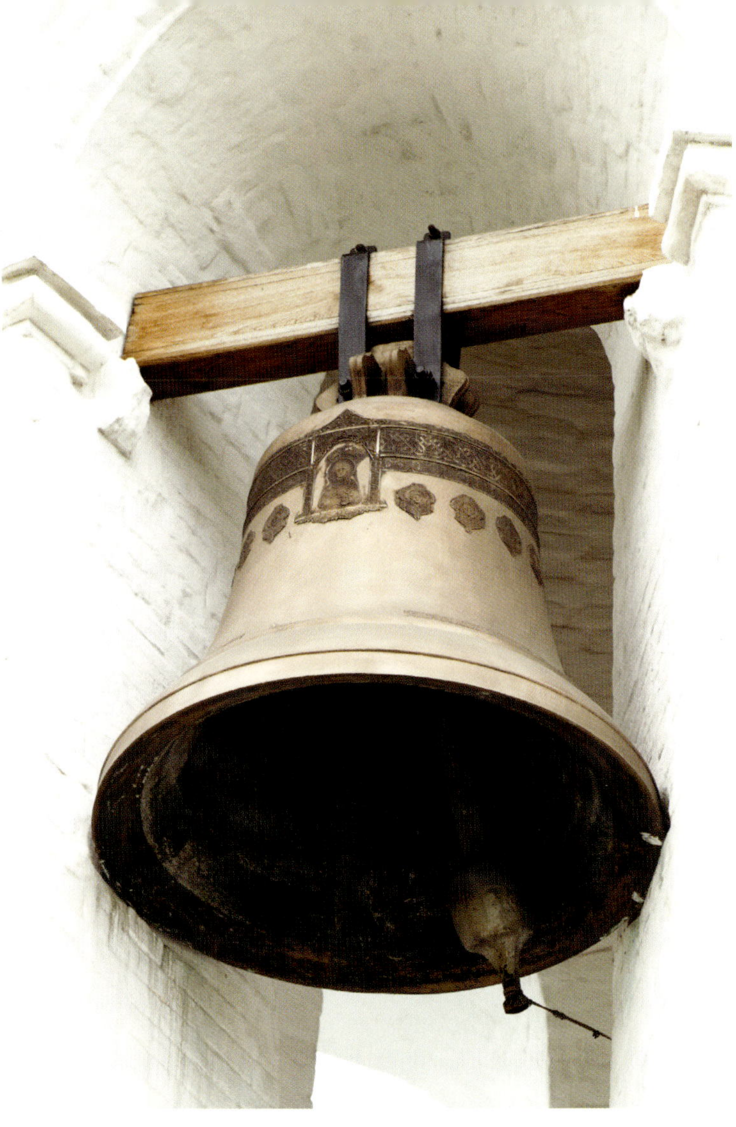

b b b b

b b b b

Bb

bed

bulb

banana

basket

back

bat

bricks

box